W9-BYA-026

Tall, Taller, Tallest

by Rebecca Felix

Ideas for Parents and Teachers

Amicus Readers let children practice reading informational texts at the earliest reading levels. Familiar words and concepts with close photo-text matches support early readers.

Before Reading

- Discuss the cover photo with the child. What does it tell him?
- Ask the child to predict what she will learn in the book.

Read the Book

- "Walk" through the book and look at the photos. Let the child ask questions.
- Read the book to the child, or have the child read independently.

After Reading

- Use the photo quiz at the end of the book to review the text.
- Prompt the child to make connections. Ask: *Can you think of other objects that are different heights?*

Amicus Readers are published by Amicus
P.O. Box 1329, Mankato, MN 56002
www.amicuspublishing.us

Copyright © 2015. International copyright reserved in all countries. No part of this book may be reproduced in any form without written permission from the publisher.

Library of Congress Cataloging-in-Publication Data
Felix, Rebecca, 1984-
  Tall, taller, tallest / Rebecca Felix.
    p. cm. -- (Size It Up!)
  K to Grade 3.
  Audience: Age 6
  ISBN 978-1-60753-579-9 (hardcover) --
ISBN 978-1-60753-617-8 (pdf ebook)
 1. English language--Adjective--Juvenile literature. 2. English language--Comparison--Juvenile literature. I. Title.
  PE1241.F467 2014
  428.2--dc23

                                    2013044011

Photo Credits: Shutterstock Images, cover (left), cover (right), 1 (left), 1 (right), 4–5, 6 (right), 8 (left), 8 (right), 9, 10 (left), 11, 12 (left), 13, 14 (left), 15, 16 (top left), 16 (bottom left), 16 (bottom right); Jorg Hackemann/Shutterstock Images, cover (middle), 1 (middle), 10 (right), 16 (bottom middle); John Brueske/Shutterstock Images, 3; Aaron Amat/Shutterstock Images, 4 (left), 16 (top right); Eric Isselee/Shutterstock Images, 5 (right), 16 (top middle); Eugene Sergeev/Shutterstock Images, 6 (left); BioLife Pics/Shutterstock Images, 7; Doug Meek/Shutterstock Images, 12 (right); Patrick Poendl/Shutterstock Images, 14 (right)

Produced for Amicus by The Peterson Publishing Company and Red Line Editorial.

Editor Jenna Gleisner
Designer Craig Hinton
Printed in the United States of America
Mankato, MN
January, 2014
PA10001
10 9 8 7 6 5 4 3 2 1

Tall objects have great height. How do the world's tallest objects compare in size?

An ostrich is a tall animal.
Elephants are taller.
Giraffes are the tallest
animals on Earth.

elephant

ostrich

4

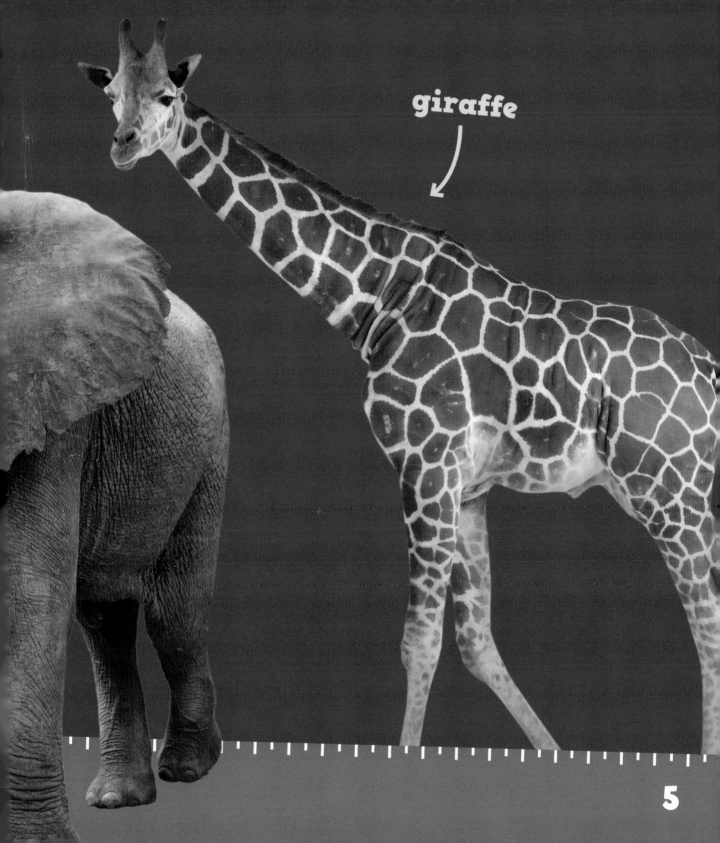

giraffe

Palm trees are tall. Giant sequoias grow taller. Coast redwoods are the tallest trees. One in California measures as tall as 20 giraffes.

giant sequoia

palm tree

coast
redwood

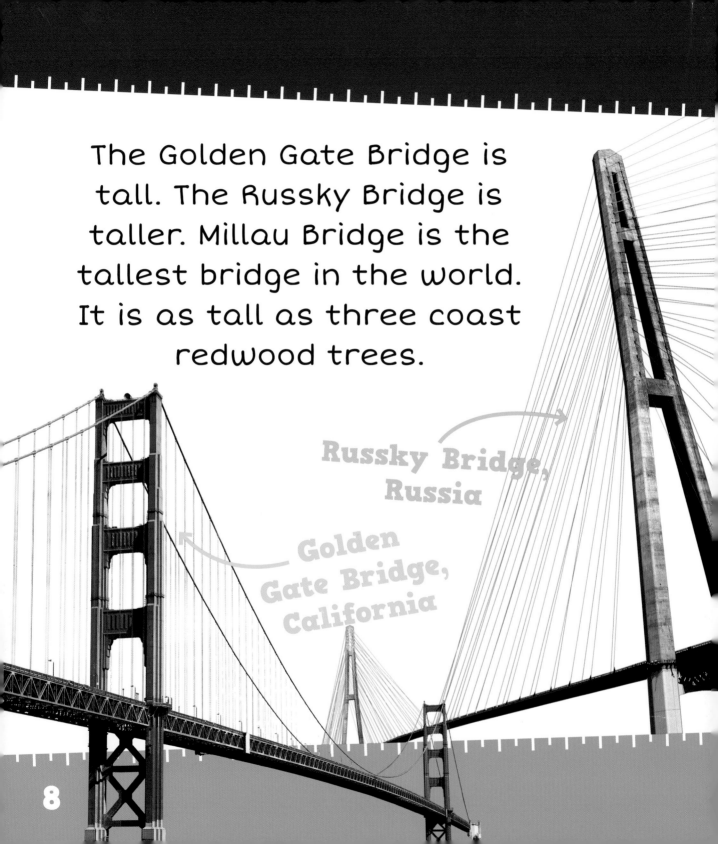

The Golden Gate Bridge is tall. The Russky Bridge is taller. Millau Bridge is the tallest bridge in the world. It is as tall as three coast redwood trees.

Russky Bridge, Russia

Golden Gate Bridge, California

Millau Bridge, France

Burj Al Arab is tall. The Empire State Building is taller. Burj Khalifa is the tallest building. It has more than 160 floors.

Empire State Building, New York

Burj Al Arab, Dubai

Burj Khalifa, Dubai

11

Niagara Falls is tall. Yosemite Falls is even taller. Angel Falls is the tallest waterfall in the world. It is almost as tall as three Millau Bridges.

Yosemite Falls, California

Niagara Falls, Canada and USA

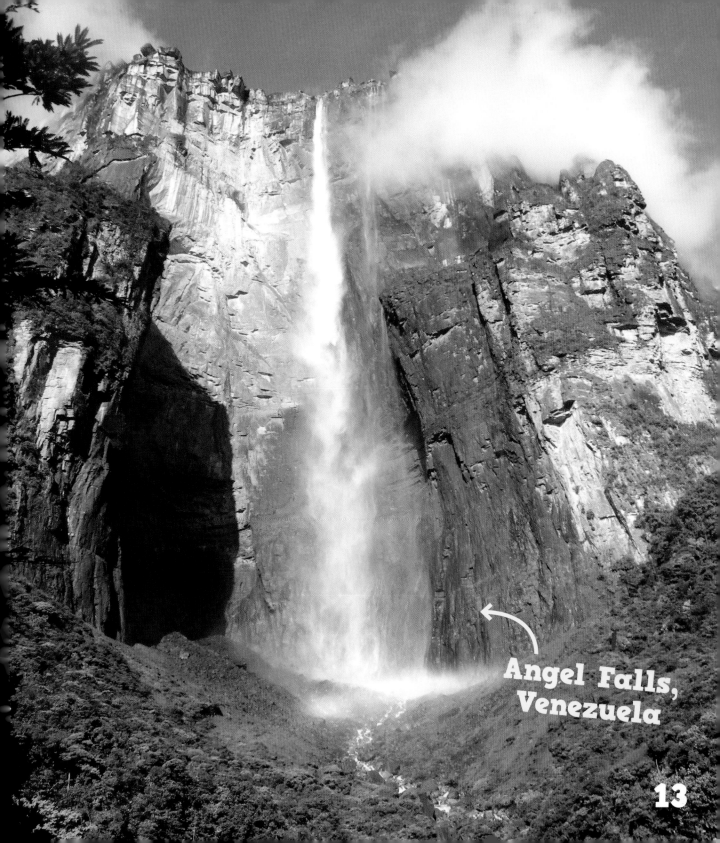

Angel Falls,
Venezuela

13

Mount McKinley is a tall mountain. K2 is taller. Mount Everest is the tallest. It is taller than nine Angel Falls waterfalls!

K2, Asia

Mount McKinley, Alaska

Mount Everest, Asia

15

Which object is the tallest in each group?

elephant

giraffe

ostrich

Burj Khalifa

Empire State Building

Burj Al Arab